I See Stupid People

Andrews McMeel Publishing, LLC

an Andrews McMeel Universal company

1130 Walnut Street, Kansas City, Missouri 64106

www.andrewsmcmeel.com

ISBN: 978-0-7407-7810-0

Library of Congress Control Number: 2008935741

11 12 13 SDB 10 9 8 7 6 5 4

Licensed by Creatif

www.coedikit.com

ATTENTION: SCHOOLS AND BUSINESSES

Andrews McMeel books are available at quantity discounts with bulk purchase for educational, business, or sales promotional use. For information, please e-mail the Andrews McMeel Publishing Special Sales Department: specialsales@amuniversal.com

I See STUPID PEOPLE

And They Are Getting On My LAST NERVE!

Cheryl Caldwell

Andrews McMeel
Publishing, LLC

Kansas City • Sydney • London

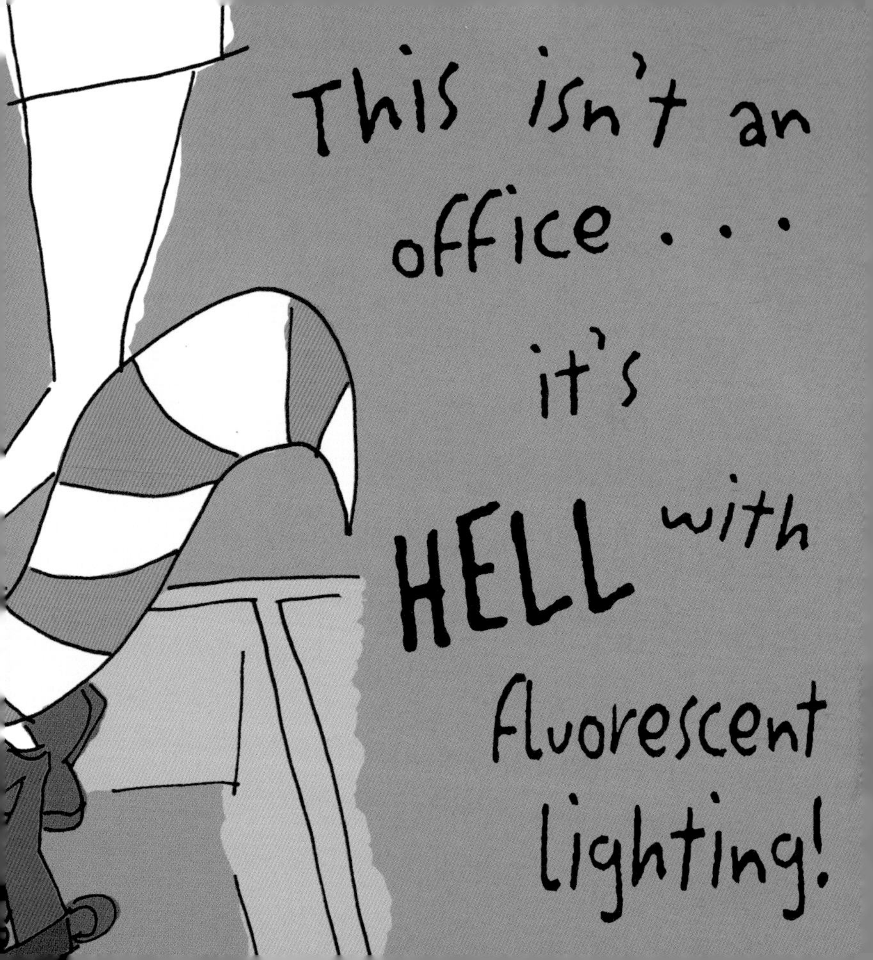
This isn't an office . . . it's HELL with fluorescent lighting!

And there's not much relief on the outside.

Life's a circus and I'm stuck in the freak tent.

You do the best you can,

When in doubt,
MUMBLE.

often outdoing yourself.

Go the extra mile.

But look whom you're working with.

I
see
stupid
people.

No matter where you turn, you're faced with insanity,

A few presents short of a full sleigh

incompetence,

ome people are like Slinkies . . .
not really good for much, but you can't help but smile when you see one tumble down the stairs.

and insolence.

I'm sorry but
I'm all out
of nice.

And yet, you're still polite to others,

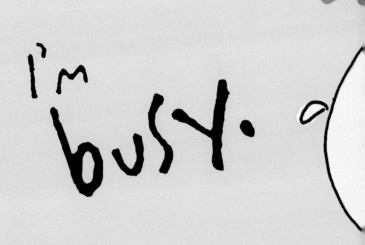

I'm busy.

and apologetic when you're not.

When I said
   you were
AVERAGE,
I was just being
   MEAN.

You inquire
about their
lives,

So when's the Wizard going to get back to you about that brain?

offer any assistance they may need,

I'll
help
you
out.

and appreciate
their
contributions.

You work well on team projects,

Great
minds
think
alike.

Unfortunately,
so do stupid ones.

regardless of whom you are working with.

I'm not a complete
idiot
—some parts are missing.

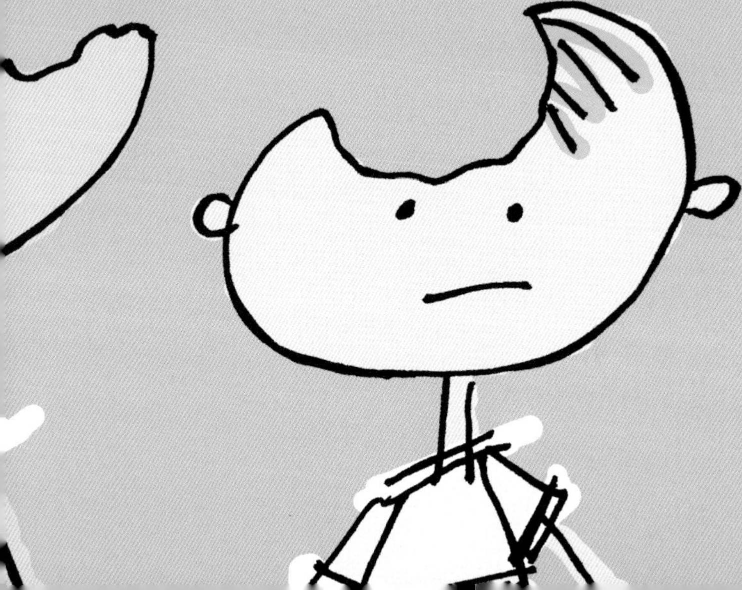

You're always an integral part of the group,

Do not follow,
    for I may not lead.

Do not lead,
    for I may not follow.

Just get away from me,
    will you!?!

often doing more than your share.

My boss said my
assignment
was a
piece of cake ...
so
I
ate
it.

You stay on task,

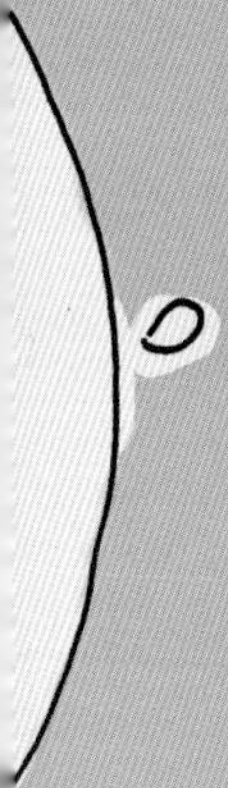

Just because
I have a
short
attention span
doesn't mean . . .

offer your many skills,

my
photographic
memory

and present your
brilliant mind.

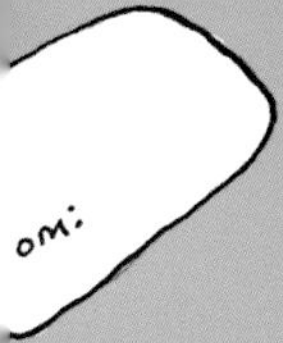

GIFTED

(certainly no one would pay for me)

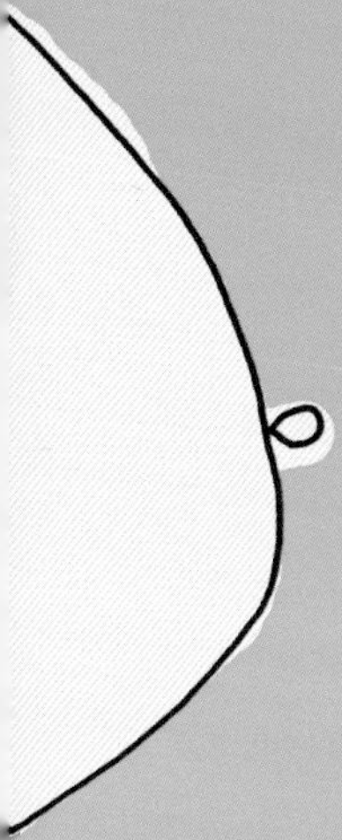

You set goals

I don't. drink anymore.

(I also don't drink any less!)

and work hard to
achieve them.

A train station is where
a train stops.

A bus station is where
a bus stops.

This is my
work station . . .

You know you should slow down.

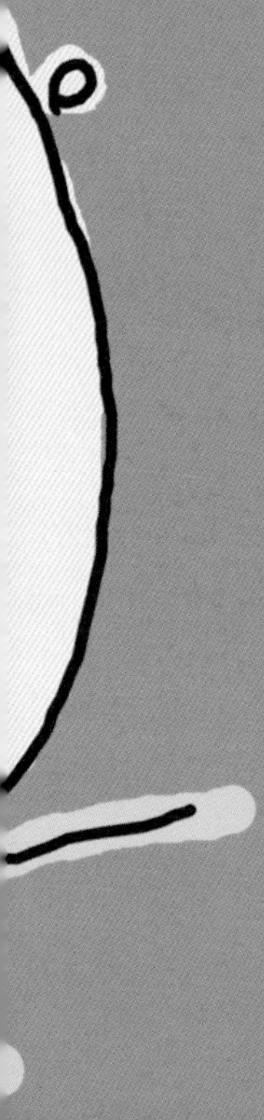

Stress
is when
You wake up
screaming . . .

and
realize
You haven't
fallen asleep
yet.

And, yet, you keep trying to do more.

shop-a-holic

Complications have gotten out of control.

It may be time for drastic
measures.

kill

me

now.

Or perhaps semidrastic measures.

Don't make me
kick you.

It can be a bit confusing at times.

Did you ever stop to think . . .

Some say it's because you do too much.

You can never garden too mulch.

But it's not your fault you have a week's worth of obligations to fit into a single day.

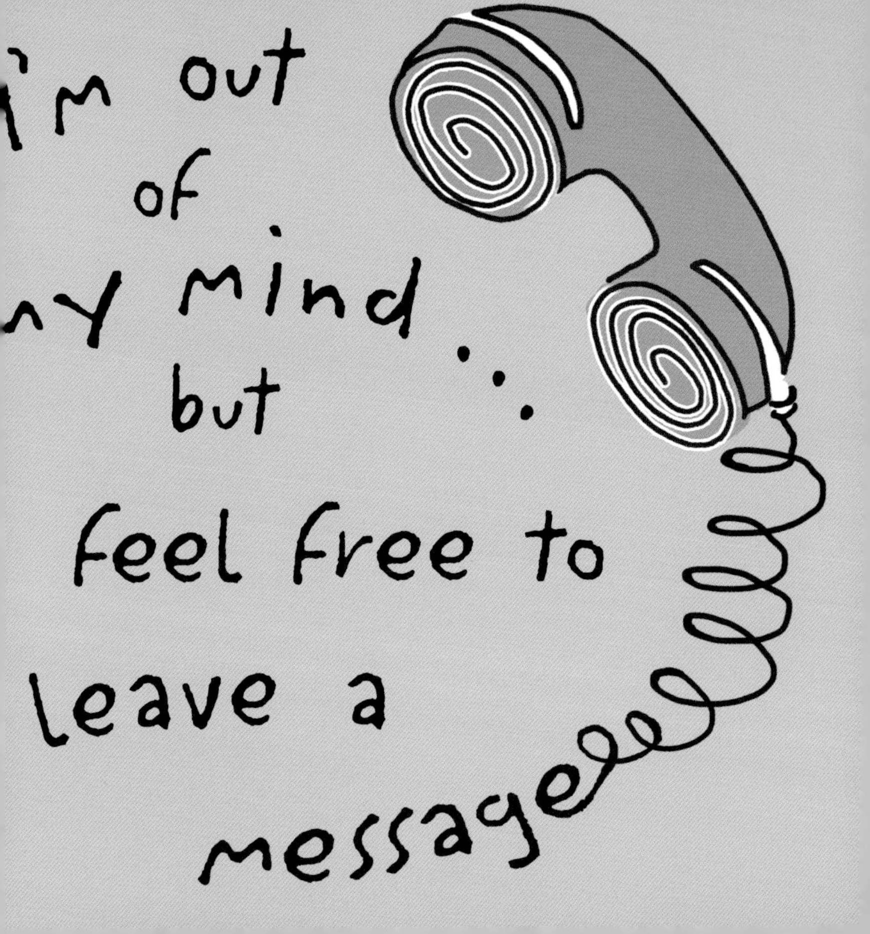
'm out
of
ny mind
but
feel free to
leave a
message

It's time to take control.

How can I
miss you
if you won't
go
away?

Perhaps you need to get away from it all.

NO
WAKE
ZONE

Take a step back and reprioritize.

Seas
the
Day

Get a new outlook on life.

Some say the glass
is half-full.
Some say the glass
is half-empty.

I say,
"Are you gonna drink that?"

Things are rarely as bad as they seem.

Before my morning coffee,

You just have to change your point of view.

Those who think small things can't

MAKE A

DIFFERENCE

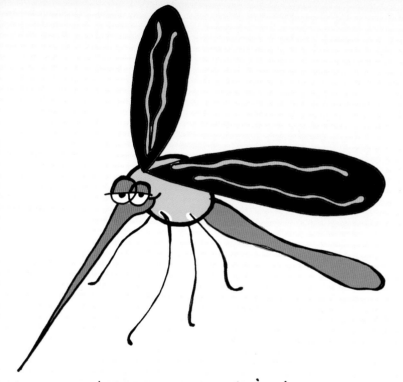

have never tried
to sleep with a mosquito.

Appreciate things for what they are.

Pain
in
the
Neck

And in the end,

Exercise,
Eat
Right,